Innovative or Passionate?

Who are you, and why are you doing this?

Regardless of your business acumen or educational background, basic concepts are necessary to launch a brand into the retail sales arena. You will struggle to reach your goal without a few essential tidbits of information or insight into potential pitfalls in an industry with more failures than successes.

Now - let's discuss the word failure; Edison and many others claimed that failing was an excellent way of learning. During my career in product and business development, over 20 years, I experienced many learning curves. Suffusive to say, far more than were imagined. Success occurred by being fortunate enough to have amazing people around me providing support and training. These teachers and mentors made the bumps in the road mere minor inconveniences. Once, it was suggested to me to reference the hurdles as Duck Bites; a duck bite is, simply put, a nuisance. It may be somewhat painful at first, and no one has (to my knowledge) ever died from one. So shrug the event aside and learn what you can from it. It doesn't define you or your career; if nothing else is to be gained by the duck bite, you, at least, have a great story to tell at a future success party.

Before jumping into the nuts and bolts, you must know little about me.

My career has spanned pharmaceutical and personal care product lines since my early twenties. Curious by nature, I loved playing with products and testing their miraculous claims. Early on, I had the privilege of working for a small company that decided to utilize its company name to brand a haircare line. Annual revenues from the salon chain generated multi-millions of dollars;

adding a product line appeared to be a natural addition to the organization. Multiple service outlets set the product up succinctly for taking a new product to market. I will return to their success story at the end of the book.

Working with the world-renowned stylist team and product line developers, I started my adventure into the world of product development. This journey provided the opportunity to take on the role of General Manager for a small personal care product manufacturer. Working in this environment provided a fantastic opportunity to learn a new industry and to garner knowledge concerning regulations and requirements for consumer-facing products. After seven years of managing this organization, the next great opportunity appeared. I took on a position as a project manager for a pharmaceutical contract manufacturing company. Although this may seem like a downgrade on the career path, it allowed me to step into a world I knew very little about and led me to discover one of the most fascinating industries in the world.

Ten years later, having worked my way up to Business Development and Project Management leader, the company had grown, and I had a vested financial interest in the future. Fortune smiled upon us when an acquisition from an international corporate brand was complete. While many of the people I worked with chose to stay and continue with the organization, I opted to move on and follow my passion. My passion, you may wonder, is to continue to grow and learn with the end goal of helping others achieve their success. A variation of Christian and Buddhist teachings has taught me something I strive for every day:

It is not what we gain in life but what we give back that provides true contentment.

To quote Helen Walton, "It's not what you gather, but what you scatter that tells what kind of life you have lived."

Before moving into the whats and hows, remember that no one does it alone. The opportunity to share my knowledge with you would never have occurred without the people along the way who taught me, pushed me, irritated me, and forced me to learn.

So who are you, and why are you doing this?

Be clear about your intent when starting this project. What's your end game look like? Create clear goals, adjust them when necessary, and be flexible on this journey, as it will consume your days, nights, and money.

Don't skip past any chapters thinking you already know best, doing so will be costly to you at some point. I say that because I experienced grave mistakes firsthand and was very lucky that no one ever died.

At the book's beginning, the questions were posed; Are you Innovative or Passionate? It is a trick question; you must be both to achieve a successful product line.

Either one, utilized by itself, will never grow a success story.

Conceptualization

It is assumed that if you are reading this book, you have an idea of a product to launch or already have and are struggling to move it forward. The first article we will address is the who, what, and how question. What makes you different?

Three key areas you need to define before going forward:

Platform, Difference, Target Audience

Platform

★ **Area of Expertise**

★ **Benefits**

★ **Science**

★ Area of expertise

If you think about it, no one wants to listen to someone who isn't an expert. There are plenty of concepts without proof in the world today. Who is going to spend their precious time on a format without validity? Well, maybe your family and close friends will, and most likely, they will walk away and hope for the best for you. That will not sell a product line! Who hasn't encountered someone who only knew half of what they were saying? Incorrect data and false assumptions will kill a product line before you ever make a pitch to start raising money.

Know what you are talking about - Be an expert!

Nothing is more embarrassing than someone who thinks they are more intelligent than you. An outsider challenging your belief system?

You must prepare to respond with compelling and well-researched information.

In my years on the front lines of the trades, I will say there is something immensely satisfying about shutting down the naysayer with factual information.

★ Benefits

How does the end user benefit? What is the value to the consumer? Why should they spend hard-earned cash on your product line?

You need, in my opinion, at least three key benefits for a consumer to make the purchase: one Major and two supportive.

The product   [Name] will [adjective] while [Claim] & [Claim].

Use this as a benchmark to build out the benefits list.

★ Science

Is their science supporting your benefits? Do you have data to prove the benefit claims?

With the internet accessible to almost everyone in the free world, the average consumer's drive to understand the products they use will drive them to research your lineup; you need scientific data to support your claims. I am referring to actual, robust, verifiable data that proves what you are saying is true. It is critical that you have this defined during the concept phase; if not, you will spend unnecessary money and time backtracking, possibly delaying that first big sale or, worse - missing that acquisition proposal.

Differentiation

Okay, you have a concept. You are set to blaze trails into the marketplace.

Hold up! What makes you unique? What makes your product line capture someone's attention? All the clever marketing in the world will not generate long-term profit.

Trust me; your marketing team will want to know what makes you unique.

And by the way, you need to hire a marketing team! I don't cover marketing as it is not my area of expertise, but if you recall, I stated earlier that you can't do it all alone; a strong marketing team is critical to support long-term growth.

Key areas of differentiation:

★ Who's going to use it?

★ Organic/Natural/Healing

★ Style

★ Price Point

★ Who's going to use it?

When the science and benefits discussion happened, a product statement should have evolved; the evolution is critical in determining your demographic profile. We will cover more of that in the next section.

★ Organic/Natural/Healing

Have you landed here in this grouping? Be Prepared!

Many factors impact these claims, which may lead to crucial market differentiators. They come with a cost. Be sure you understand the impact on your costs if this is part of your plan. From manufacturing to material costs, the end price you will pay for the product will be substantially more than products not making these claims. I am not making any judgment on this path. I personally steer towards organic and naturally derived products; they are a healthy choice, in my opinion. I bring this up merely as there is an impact on the cost. This is crucial information to your COGS; you need to know this while developing your financial plans.

★ Style

I am willing to bet money you are thinking,

"What the hell could style have to product conceptualization?"

Believe it or not, you predetermined a look or style the moment you started thinking about this product. You have pictured the tall, sleek glass bottle with white and black print, topped off with a perfect white rubber dropper for dispensing. All packed into a beautiful satiny soft-touch box that feels great in your hands.

Ok, that's probably an exaggeration, but the reality is you have seen a product that you will want to emulate their style. It's human nature, and quite frankly, when starting up, it's wise to copy existing product looks. It will be easier to get into production. However, with that idea hidden in the back of your head, be sure the style suits the product going inside.

If the product color is milky white, do you want a clear bottle so the consumer can see when it has been consumed? Is there something special in the product that needs to show through the packaging?

Just like the style in your home should flow and be consistent and inviting (according to the designers on TV), so should your product presentation.

Think about it, put it down on paper, and research what others in your category are doing; you may want to go 180 degrees away from them for differentiation (as long as it's functional, that is a great option).

★ Price Point

Price Point is one of the most critical parts to establish for your product. Where are you going to sit on the market price scale?

If pricing is a planned point of differentiation, this should be determined now, as it will impact every path you choose going forward. If you are looking to upset the market at a low entry price, there are other differences you may have to omit.

If your price point targets high-end consumers and only them, be prepared to face the challenges of finding quality manufacturers working with small-scale productions.

★ Target Audience

As mentioned above, who is going to use the product? It is imperative that you have clearly defined your target audience.

Is it a disease state your product will heal?

Focusing on the reduction of irritation for an ailment? Youth and Beauty?

The list can quickly become very long; you must narrow it down to two or three attributes. Once you have established the need for the consumer, you need to answer the fundamental questions:

- ✓ **Who**
- ✓ **What**
- ✓ **When**
- ✓ **Where**

✓ **Who**

This appears to be an elementary question. Not so fast; according to the 2017 Consumer Expenditures report, the average American spent 60K on consumer goods. Stop and do the math here; if the average annual income across the US is $70K (according to the same report by the Bureau of Labor Statistics), the average consumer is spread thin financially. Logically we know this, but we tend to put this detail passionately aside.

It is critical that you know WHO is going to buy your product, plain and simple. You must know who the consumer is if you are to persuade them to give up something else they purchase to buy your product. This begs the question, are you focusing on niche or mass markets?

✓ What

Now on to What are they going to buy? Your product - of course. But what size? How will it be delivered from the container? Is it a cream, a lotion, or an aqueous solution? How much should they use each time? Is it colored by nature? Will it stain if it does have color? And on and on and on.

You see where this is going; not one detail about the product can be undetermined.

✓ When

The When. Establish a launch date and work backward from that date to see if the intended release date is realistic. Develop a Gantt Chart to see how you get to launch. [A Gantt Chart is an established list of tasks with timing for due dates.] The Chart will continuously evolve,   and be aware that variables will occur; a failed test can set you back several weeks if not months. Be realistic that "Next Week" is never an option when launching a product line.

On a side note, if you are working with a supplier that doesn't offer Project Management as part of the process, you may want to move on. A PM group is critical to the manufacturing process, a standard in the industry, and an invaluable tool to ensure you reach the end game as planned. The cost for this is part of the overheads for a supplier, be cautious about paying for a service that should be part of the offerings from your supplier.

✓ Where

This one will trip you up; it's not about where you will sell. Selling is indeed essential data to have as it will drive the Where being addressed here; this is about the fulfillment of your products.

Your plan to manage shipping and handling is important to determine now. Do you plan to do it yourself (out of your garage) or work with a large distribution partner such as Amazon or Shopify? A later section is dedicated to Fulfillment and the details you need to know about.

I assume that you are probably feeling a bit overwhelmed by now. Should you not come from a manufacturing or development background, and I am guessing if you did, you wouldn't have invested in this book, there is a lot to know. All that said, remember what we stated earlier -

"no one does it all alone!"

Find the right partners to work with, this is critical to your success.

Classifications

Selling to the public requires your Brand to follow consumer protection laws; steer clear of unsubstantiated claims. You don't want a reputation of being an infamous Snake Oil salesman. The integrity of your business is critical; this is your calling card and determines if people will be repeat customers. Once you have earned market share, please don't give it away with false substantiations for your product.

The FDA and various other government agencies regulate what may be stated about the products in the marketplace. Depending on where your product line resides within this matrix, it has been pre-determined what you can and cannot claim and how/where you can sell it. As with all things from the government, there is much room for interpretation; when it comes to interpretation, applying integrity to the equation is the best solution.

Let's touch on the four consumer regulatory groups familiar to most. If none of these fit the product, you are looking to launch, research, and contact a field consultant to help you. I strongly advise you have a staff member or consultant help you with these; the impact of a false claim can kill your business or, worse yet, put you in jail.

There are three basic categories of pharmaceutical products. The fourth category captures just about all other topical products.

★ **Drug**

★ **OTC**

★ **Medical Device**

★ **Personal Care/Cosmetics**

★ Drug

Products within this category will require a prescription for use from a Doctor or other qualified medical personnel. They will include the symbols "R" or "Rx," along with instructions for use [IFU] and possibly compounding instructions for a qualified pharmacist.

★ OTC

Over-the-Counter drugs are regulated by the FDA and approved for use by a consumer without a prescription. The FDA has clearly defined what you can and can't say in regard to the product's efficacy as well as the level of the active ingredient acceptable for the application. OTCs are monitored jointly by the FDA and the product manufacturer via regular audits and correspondence between the two groups mentioned above.

★ Medical Device

Medical Devices also fall under FDA guidance, however, under a different platform. Combination OTC/Medical Devices exist and land in their own regulatory domain. These products are meant to serve a mechanical function of types. Medical devices are best known as implants, apparatus, implements, Etc. That said, topical medical devices do exist; they serve in a reactive, somewhat mechanical way. It is far more scientific than that, but you get the idea. The path for a med-device can be quite expensive to develop unless a predicate device exists that will support the claims you are choosing to make.

★ Personal Care/Cosmetics

My sense is that most people reading this book will fall into this category; this is a logical starting point for launching a product line. This category is the catch-all for products utilized on people: external body application - hair, skin, or nails.

Random quiz - What's the largest organ of the body?

Personal Care products are not allowed to make claims that fall under FDA guidelines. For example, you cannot say, "Prevents sun damage." This statement is a sunscreen claim. Keywords to not use are: prevents, heals, cures. If these are in your sales vocabulary arsenal, consult a regulatory agent to understand exactly what you are selling and what is acceptable to promote the product.

Simply put, if you can buy at a salon, spa, or retail establishment, it will most likely fall into the personal care category.

With proper testing and documentation, marketing claims are appropriate. However, don't say it if you can't substantiate it. You may believe the claim to be valid, but trust me, someone will find a reason to challenge your interpretation. You should have data to take the wind out of their sail, not the wind out of your sales.

Regulatory Compliance

Now you are thinking, what is this? Not another hurdle to jump through!

Afraid so, another hurdle to climb over. Don't give up; this is just part of the process of putting a safe, efficacious, and adored product on the end user's shelf.

I am going to provide an overview of Clinical Studies and Registrations quickly. While these are predominately utilized in the Pharma world, they have value for cosmetics. With consumer access to the web and all the information it contains (both true and false), consumers are becoming self-appointed product watchdogs. While this may be well-intended, it can kill a product line if you are not adequately prepared for rebuttal should an attack occur.

I know a company that a well-known consumer advocate magazine took on. The magazine reported incorrect information to consumers, severely impacting the company's brand. The good news is that the brand had the data to push back and received a retraction on the inaccurate information.

★ **Clinical Studies**

★ **Registrations**

★ **Clinical Studies**

Here is where you will gather the information you need to make the claims you want to make about your product. Many companies perform these services, from basic tests such as irritation testing or moisturizing competence to more in-depth analyses such as SPF ratings.

The value of this testing is two-fold:

1. Ensure your product is working as you intended

2. Meet compliance with regulatory agencies

If the product falls into the Pharma/Med Device world, there are specific tests that are required. Mentioned above is SPF; this would be a requirement of the FDA for the claim of the protection factor and how long it is effective. A clinical testing site lab would most likely have protocols to ensure the requirements are met and therefore are part of the support chain you will need.

Products in the cosmetic/personal care category don't generally require clinical testing. That said, go back to your differentiation list and see what tests might be used to enhance and/or support what you want to say. This investment can add much weight to the marketplace. Testing can be costly, be prepared and be open to options offered by your contract manufacturer or testing facility for alternative means to accomplish the end goal.

Depending on your risk tolerance, the product can go to market with the bare minimum testing. However, I strongly advise you to understand what your competitors are doing and let that guide you to the minimum standard you apply. Even though federal regulations may only require a basic test, if all your competition is doing three tests to support claims, you want to buck up and meet them at their level. Add an additional claim if you can; your marketing team will appreciate it.

Above all else, don't fudge your data to make your product look better than it is. Market Integrity is crucial for success. If you are just seeking to make money, I suggest you enter into financial trading and not risk hurting another human being (or animal, for that matter) to make a buck. The best example to give you on this topic is to share about a company that failed to comply with regulatory agencies and continued misleading the public. They are responsible for taking the life of a two-year-old child by supplying a medical product that failed to meet safety specifications. The impact ultimately shut the company down, and thousands of people were put out of work. The owners were prosecuted, losing all their material possessions. Taking a life for a dollar bill is not the Karma I believe you want.

★ Registrations

Depending on the classification the product falls under will drive what registrations are necessary. If the product is deemed cosmetic, there are few regulatory registrations required. Your manufacturer will maintain all the records of production [record of manufacturing]; these are necessary for when a product audit occurs.

Drug and Medical Device registrations are complex and should be managed by your manufacturer. Ultimately, they are your front line of defense against the FDA, and you should keep it that way. Work with someone you can trust and let them do their job accordingly. Hire a third-party auditor to hold them accountable and work with someone who runs their business like yours.

It bears repeating, *you can't do this alone.*

Regulatory consultants are necessary if you are a small company. Plan the consulting expense ahead of time. If you don't know one, use a resource such as Linked In to connect with resources. This may sound overwhelming if you are a startup, and yes, the initial expense is not cheap, but the recovery period should be relatively short. The category you fall into will determine the level of cost; for cosmetic products, it should be reasonably low as you only need the basics covered to ensure you aren't saying anything you are not allowed to claim. The other end of the spectrum is the Drug classification; it is quite costly and has recurring costs, most of which repeat annually.

Development

I am sure you are wondering why this category is so far down the list, and you're probably right, as you already have a product in mind that is ready to go! I am going to say, once again, Hold Up!

Yes, you may have developed the product, per se, but I am willing to bet you have not gone through the rigors necessary to move that product into manufacturing beyond your kitchen or garage. We are going to outline three essential events that must occur before you can sell your product.

★ **Safety Testing**

★ **Shelf Life**

★ **Active Testing**

As I eluded to earlier, the last thing you want to do with your product is to harm anyone. While some allergies and variables are outside the control of the developer and manufacturer, the basics should be covered to give the best foot forward as possible. In addition to the testing already outlined, these next three are imperative to complete before product leaves your warehouse.

★ Safety Testing

During product development, specific criteria must be established. These standards must be repeatable and clearly defined every time the product is produced. This will include such things as microbial count, absence of yeast and mold, and Active levels. (Active levels are for Drugs and OTC products, cosmetic products will not have active level claims). Bugs (microorganisms) can grow in weird places;

testing is necessary to ensure consumer safety.

If this is news to you, seek assistance understanding and developing this critical data.

★ Shelf Life

How long is your product suitable for use? How long can it set on the shelf before losing potency or becoming a messy goo of oil and water, aka separation?

Will it hold up in the trunk of a car in Phoenix during August? Is it still applicable to the skin after sitting on a doorstep in Toronto in January?

During the development phase, the product should be stressed under varying man-made conditions to determine how long it is usable and under what conditions. This information will help assess Expiration dating for Drug/OTC/MedDevice products.

One can also establish PAO [period after opening] dating utilizing these methods for personal care items; personal care items do not require this testing in the US, but it is highly recommended. The data provide additional data for stock replenishment planning purposes.

Global testing requirements vary for shelf-life dating: this is where defining the Who you are selling to comes into play. Testing for several different climate zones may be necessary for your product to be shipped internationally. The requirement for international testing shifts significantly by country or union, be in the know.

★ Active Testing

This section only applies to products making claims per FDA regulations. I cannot think of a single reason for a cosmetic product to require active testing. Something is off if you are told this is a requirement for your product. You must dig further into the reasoning and find a resource to determine the disconnect.

For any drug - OTC or Prescription - the level of an active ingredient must be tested every time the product is manufactured. The development process and regulatory guidance determine the Active level. This may follow an established protocol for an active ingredient commonly used, and that's OK! Just know that this must be verified and proven before going to market. Avoid developing new testing methods if at all possible, as this is quite expensive; sometimes, there is no way around it, but you should at least ask if it's possible to utilize an existing method and then verify its functionality.

To close this chapter out, here is some discouraging news - except for cosmetics, all products must have their safety testing completed before market launch. This means you need a minimum of eighteen months' worth of pilot batch material data before starting the manufacturing process for commercial sales. Cosmetics don't require lengthy testing; however, please note that you cannot apply the PAO dating without some significant risk. If you aren't sure - contact a risk management consultant for clarification.

Manufacturing

Finally, we are to the part you assume will be the easiest.

Visualize loud horns honking and lights flashing about now!

Finding the right manufacturing partner is not an easy task. With the knowledge you have garnered this far, you know enough questions to ask the manufacturing salesman. The answers provided should provide you a sense of whether to pursue them or not. From having worked in both small, midsize, and large manufacturing, it is without a doubt not about the size of the facility. What you need is someone who knows what they are doing and how you will support a business relationship long term.

Moving a product once you have established production within a facility is incredibly expensive. The hurdles are numerous - so ask your proposed supplier to take you on a "date." Get to know them, understand how they will treat you, what level of integrity do they have, and, most importantly, whether they have been in trouble with the FDA or the IRS. Don't run away if they have; just ask the reasons and use your gut instincts to determine whether they responded truthfully. Of course, you will then go forward and verify the details before moving in with them, so to speak.

Key bits to discuss with your supplier:

MOQ's, Services, Terms

★ MOQ's

Minimum Order Quantities requirements are essential to understand if you and your potential supplier are a good fit. Most companies launching a new product need small quantities to start. There is no reason to plan 1 million units on the first order; that has financial ruin all over it.

Depending on whether you are transferring from a development lab to a manufacturer or utilizing an all-in-one facility, your first orders will, most likely, be somewhat small. Ask if they can accommodate scale-up (pilot) batches and their range of kettle sizes. The size ranges will help you translate what a typical order size will produce. Do some basic math and understand the translation of kilograms to ounces; this will be the best Google search you will ever use.

Facilities often have different equipment available to fill the product into its container. Some are automated and have high minimum run requirements, whereas some offer semi-automated or manual fill-ing. The high-speed machines will get you a better price per unit but stop and think: can I sell that number of units before it is no longer usable? The lower volumes are more conducive to start with, in my opinion. Allow yourself some flexibility for small runs in the early part of the launch. What if the color is off or consumers don't like the aroma? Plan to make changes if necessary for market success. With that said, don't run to change something every-time a consumer has a preference challenge for you. Some people in the marketplace will not like what you are selling.

Your manufacturer will have costs associated with changing equipment or producing larger volumes; be sure to clarify the charges. When it is time to move to the high-speed machines, the price for change-parts and/or validations may offset the savings and not make sense at first. Understanding your growth patterns will help you determine when the change is necessary.

Lastly, be prepared to let your future partner know your business plan. Communicate with your account executive the expected growth plan, your marketing targets, Etc. Remember, you want this to be a partnership for the long haul.

★ Services

Manufacturing services will vary by each company. Developing your product and regulatory requirements may narrow the scope of whom you can work with. I suggest attending a manufacturing trade show to get a feel for whom you might like to build a relationship. There are several events in the US annually, along with international options. It may make sense to produce outside the USA, depending on your long-term plans. If you are this far along with a project, resources should be available to recommend shows or people to contact. Your packaging supplier, chemical vendor, unit carton guy - any one of the people you have talked with should know who is around that may provide support for your project.

Once you have established contact, either at a trade show or via a sales call, inquire about their services. Do they only fill and package products? What are their minimum testing requirements? Perhaps they have a lab and can provide in-house release testing before shipping. Ask if they offer compliance or development services. If you are small and just starting a one-stop shop is your best bet as they can walk you through each of the processes and help you achieve success. Your success is also their success. Steer away from Web/Email conversations. You want to develop a relationship; person-to-person contact is critical. Determine what their project management team is like. Do they have one, and how do they manage the commercialization process? Procurement services are a must in my mind; can they handle the process turn-key? In my years of doing this work, I have yet to see a customer who could supply materials cheaper than a full-scale manufacturer can. Yes, the manufacturer will take a margin on this activity, but be guaranteed that if you calculate person-hours, shipping, invoicing, and all the "do it yourself" events - you are losing money.

Again - No one does it all alone.

The one big hiccup in all of these conversations is the cost. Expect to pay for these add-on services, one way or another. Remember, the manufacturer is in business whose intent is to be profitable, just like you. If you have done your homework and understand your business model thoroughly, you should already know what to pay for the individual unit or, more concisely, what you can afford to pay.

★ Terms

How is your business partner structured? How will they let you pay them for the work? Cash, Credit, BitCoin?

Experience suggests that a newcomer to a facility will be asked to pay a deposit before work begins, and payment is due before the product will ship. Some may offer a 50% advance payment with the balance due 30 days after shipping. If you have established a good relationship with their team and have good credit and a well-established business plan, this is a worthwhile question to ask early on. On average, plan on one year of the existing terms before asking to negotiate the terms (provided you have reordered at least once in that time frame). Remember that you will have to request changes in Terms to get them.

Going into a project like this without funding or a significant amount of cash available is, to be frank, a waste of your time. Don't give up if you have a great idea or product that will change the world. Go out and ask for money from an investor if you don't have it. Don't be shy -

Success is formed out of

_____ &

_____!

Fulfillment

Fulfillment, should you not be familiar with the term, is simply where the products will be stored and how they will move to your end-user.

In this section, we will touch base on various options and means to get your product where it needs to go. By establishing whether you will function as a B2B or B2C (touched on in the sales chapter and will be more clearly defined later on in the book), fulfillment requirements will be reasonably simple to establish.

Many companies offer services to support shipping to your customer, which is excellent, but be mindful of what your business needs are to ensure you get the most bang for your buck. Each piece of the fulfillment cycle has a fee; don't pay for services not needed.

Principal areas of focus are:

★ Type

★ MOQ

★ Services

★ Terms

★ Type

First, decide if you want to perform the fulfillment services in-house. To clarify, In-House should not be a codeword for your garage. IF you have space and understand all the bits that go with this, and you are selling cosmetics, garage fulfillment is undoubtedly an option but not highly recommended. There may be a tremendous financial reason why you choose to do this but keep that information close as it may severely impact who will do business with you. Also, it should go without saying, but ensure products are not sitting next to greasy car parts or subjected to critters.

Garage fulfillment takes organizational skills and a commitment to cleanliness. For a small business starting out selling short runs, it may be the best option for you, but I implore you to take the time to compare the costs of labor and overhead to that of a fulfillment house. Make sure this suits your business model and represents your company appropriately.

Most fulfillment centers are environmentally controlled and have the means to move things quickly and without damage. Based on your development studies, the controls for the environment may be a critical decision factor. A controlled facility is a must for any drug or medical device.

The product's regulatory status will help define what controls are necessary.

★ MOQ

As we looked at MOQs for manufacturing, a fulfillment center will have a minimum order requirement. Correctly identifying stock levels can be tricky with both inbound and outbound activities occurring. They will have criteria for the minimum quantity required in their system and a minimum for what they will ship to the customer. The business model you have set up will be key in driving this decision. Bear in mind - smaller quantities being shipped outbound (single units) will most likely incur higher costs.

An important part to know is their Turn-Time; how long will it take them to process a shipping request and put it into transit? The turn-time is most likely governed by the size and quantity of what is shipping. Know what is going to be expected by your customer. If your competitors are doing everything the next day - you need a partner who can manage next-day shipping if you want to compete.

In addition to the cost of packing up and shipping the product, there will be fees for product storage while waiting for shipping directions. The charges will vary depending on the product requirements (go back to shelf-life testing for reference). If your product requires special handling conditions, an increase in storage cost is likely. If your product cannot be stored below freezing or in a room above 50 degrees - the center needs to know this information so they may quote appropriately.

★ Services

Fulfillment centers are in abundance around the country. Their services will vary based on their target audience; if they focus on Pharma, services will most likely cover the FDA standards and the transportation tracking necessary to maintain compliance. If focused on the personal consumer market, don't expect in-depth monitoring for expiry dating without paying for the service. Understanding where your product line lies in the supply chain will save you money by not overpaying for services that aren't necessary. For example, if your product doesn't require controlled conditions, why pay for an air-conditioned warehouse in the Northeast? Don't pay for controlled shipping services with pedigree stamps if the product is not a drug. While these items may appear to be great marketing tools, the impact on your COGS can kill your profit margin. With all this in mind, three critical services from any fulfillment center will make your day-to-day operations less stressful: Billing, Inventory Control, and Reporting.

You are trusting your goods [goods equal cash] to a third party. They must have robust systems in place to track your inventory at all times. If you are unaware of how fast your product is moving out the door, you won't reorder in time from your manufacturer. This will likely create a backorder situation. As mentioned earlier, backorders are a great way to kill your business and/or your relationship with your supplier. It is unrealistic to expect your supplier to jump through hoops every time you run short on stock. Occasionally, incidents will occur, requiring a request to your supplier to pull you out of a ditch. Keep in mind if every order is a recovery mission, you become the boy who cried wolf, thereby severely impacting the relationship with your supplier. This behavior has a cost; fees and guaranteed frustration for everyone involved are possible.

All three services are integral and shouldn't exist without the other. Be aware of this critical failure point.

★ Terms

And lastly, how do you get paid? Just as in manufacturing, the cash flow process will impact your day-to-day decisions. It has been my experience that fulfillment houses will invoice the shipment on your behalf; that's great as it's one less step you have to take. But——- how is the money going to move around? Will they collect the sale, deduct their fees, and then send you a check? Sounds easy enough, right? Be cautious on this platform as your cash is delayed by X number of days; be mindful of how you write this part of the contract with them. Another scenario could be that you control freight cost by direct billing from a carrier for each shipment; this is tricky because now you will have an invoice to pay outside the fulfillment center. It may also impact your overheads as you will likely have an additional person on the payroll to manage all this.

I would venture to say this is the trickiest relationship and contract you will enter into (outside of shelving fees and automated discounts), so proceed with caution. For a small business, fulfillment services are an excellent tool if executed properly.

Be mindful of what you need and how you will benefit from their services.

Business Model

So by this point, you are thinking, why are we just now thinking about business models? Shouldn't this have been addressed a long time ago?

The answer is easy; you have been doing it all along!

Working through the steps above, you have been unknowingly laying the groundwork for how your business model will work. In each section, we have noted critical elements for running a profitable business and launching a successful product line. If you are as smart as I believe you are, you realize all pieces are intertwined. The goal has been to provide critical information for the product; now, use what you have learned to build the business.

This Chapter is extensive and very high-level. Each piece here is essential for success; if you don't understand something, hire the right person to help you with it!

Remember—–-

No one does it all alone!

Write it down!

N___ _____ _____ it a___ _____!

Here's what we are going to touch on:

★ B2B or B2C

★ Funding

★ Launchpad

★ Projections

★ Profitability

★ B2B or B2C

In short, it is critical that you understand who is going to purchase your products. The end-user decision impacts many of the things touched on earlier.

B2B, simply put: you are working with other businesses who are responsible for placing the product into the customer's hands. Think grocery store to a consumer; your organization will never actually process the sale to the end consumer. It is essential information as you need to build out your COGS to support a profit while also allowing the "sales organization" room for margin.

B2C, you are the sales organization. This model has you dealing directly with the consumer. Larger profit margins are likely; however, expenses are also higher. This model is a perfect niche for a local sales market. Unless you have the excess cash flow or a very generous banker, seek guidance setting up a niche product model. The niche market is a wonderful organic approach to growth, which is often appealing to investors but usually has heavy investment costs on the front end.

Both scenarios require support systems to be in place. As they vary in their needs, be clear about how you will support the sales of your product line. The cost to drive these models differ significantly as well. B2B requires a higher level of marketing interaction and governance to present the right message about your product. B2C involves some form of a sales force; a significant amount of investment is required to manage a sales force independently. We will discuss this more in Chapter 8.

In the B2B world, it is relatively standard for retailers to charge a fee for space on their shelves. The more prominent *The Space* - the more costly the rent will be. As this is the norm, be aware and plan your costing accordingly. Another common practice that can severely impact your profit is automated discounts, which you have no control over. It is not unusual for a retailer to begin discounting products by as much as 30% if the stated turn time isn't met. For example, if your product sits on a shelf for 90 days without sales, they have the option to place it on a discount without notifying you. As you might surmise, if you only have a small margin, you are now losing money.

★ Funding

How will you fund your business? Did a family member pass, leaving you a nice sum of cash, and now you are ready to follow your dream? Maybe you sold your Amazon stock at the right time and have a nice bankroll to drive the project. Whatever the reason for taking this on, remember there are costs beyond your expectations. That realization probably has occurred if you have made it this far in the book.

Please don't fret, it's a reality, and success requires risk.

There are, basically, two ways you are going to fund your business: Investors or Self.

Having investors is easy; it might be a bank loan or a Private Equity group. Maybe friends who believe in your actions will provide enough cash to drive the project. Wherever the support comes, remember you have an obligation to re-pay these investors and provide them with a profit for utilizing their money. Be cautious of how you manage this; many families and friends have become es-tranged over lost money or failed expec-tations.

I highly recommend you watch an episode or two of Shark Tank to garner a sense of how intense investor discussions can be, and they just touch the surface. All avenues are great options; know that you now answer to other people for your de-cisions.

You may wonder why bank loans are here in this category; simply put, commercial bankers have a commitment to protect their investors. They will want to know every detail about how you run your busi-ness. They will require progress reports and place covenants on your business performance. Again, this is not a bad thing. A partner adding experience to something you may not know should be viewed as a value add. Commercial lending is stringent for a startup unless you have invested significant amounts of your money in the business. The Bankers want to be sure you have skin in the game.

Self Funding means you have the cash to do it all on your own and will maintain all the control; awesome if you can do it! However, cash is king! Make sure you have the cash flow to support the many variables that may occur. Can you manage 90 days without cash coming? Will you have enough cash to make payroll and pay your vendors? Thinking of that 150K credit line available, do you want to tap into that? Excellent to have a credit line available but use it with caution; credit comes with a cost, and while some of it may be tax-deductible, it all comes due eventually.

Last thing in funding, and this is just a personal observation, never put your home up as collateral on a business adventure. While people will tell you this is an excellent way to support your growth, what's your backup plan if the business fails? At the time of this writing, Equity loans had a significantly higher interest rate than a standard loan; check this out and be aware of the loan cost before making this move. Perhaps you are not opposed to the risk and are willing to take the gamble; I strongly suggest against it. Talk to a commercial banker before doing that; if your business is in shape to survive, whatever the challenge is, a bank will be happy to loan you money and make interest. If they say no, chances are you need to evaluate what you are doing intensely. Better to fail at the business than to put your family out on the street.

★ Launchpad

Establishing a launchpad is critical to your business performance. What can you do to ensure people know your excellent "fountain of youth" product exists and why they need it?

As the world around us shifts to online purchases and reliance on social media influencers to drive product sales, it is vital to develop your plan to get noticed.

Having established whether you will be B2B or B2C will help drive this. Regardless, deciding how much money you are willing to invest in a marketing budget would be best. Determining which social media lanes you will use is necessary to earn product recognition and placement. Media Influencers are a must to drive product sales in the current market. Back in the day, you sent a nice note and a sample to Oprah, got a quick spot on her show, and boom, you were on your way to success. In today's market, there are a plethora of well-known influencers who can provide you with the same visibility. What do you do if you don't know anybody famous? Get to know them. Start following them on Instagram or Twitter. Engage with them, and find a way to interact with them. Develop a relationship with the people most likely to support your cause; don't just show up on their doorstep (literally and figuratively) and make the ask. You will most like be unfriended or unfollowed, and despair will consume you. If you have the savvy to be a social influencer - get out there and get known;

however, be sure you have followed all the steps of product integrity noted earlier or be guaranteed someone will call you out on it or possibly worse - sue you.

Now, the money side of launching a product.

You have paid for your development and testing. The necessary tests and registrations are complete, and your bank account is a little leaner than when you started the process.

So now you have to give the product away. Now you are saying to yourself, WHAT????

Yes, it's true; you have to give a lot of products away for people to test and begin to write outstanding reviews for you. It is a reality in today's market; one of the first stops made after a product has caught someone's attention is an internet review site. If you don't have sufficient claims of greatness from users - you better have the budget of a pharmaceutical giant. Whether doing an independent location to sell directly or utilizing a retailer, giveaways are a must. The cost belongs to your marketing budget and nowhere else. The old adage that the more you give, the more you get is most assuredly true in the product world. Be creative about how you do it; don't just throw it in someone's bag as an add-on and hope they use it! Create a prize giveaway or gift with purchase. Offer a free sample size when the customer joins your email list or offer a discount for first-time buyers.

Samples submitted to your influencers should be a full-size containers, don't be cheap. Pay attention to what other companies are doing to create market buzz.

Make a budget and start your launch efforts as soon as you have completed development; you don't want to wait to have the product in hand before you start telling people about it. Perhaps your supplier can produce some lab samples to begin the process. Perhaps that pilot batch you paid for during the testing phase has proven stable and can be filled into small containers for sampling. Utilize your supplier to help you with this crucial piece of marketing.

One final note on this, unless you are a trained graphic designer, don't design your brand and marketing materials.

What's the key point here ---

No _____ _____ __ _____ _____!

★ Projections

Through all your hard work and passion, you have spent hours determining who needs this and why they will use it. By understanding the product's key attributes and your demographic audience, you can quickly establish what to sell the product for and how many units you can sell per year. Sales are how we measure the success of a product line, but that is not just about units moved; it also indicates profitability for a brand. Be wary of having huge sales dollars with low-profit dollars. Earlier, I mentioned Cash is King, if you want to enjoy the fruits of your labors, profit dollars are necessary.

Projections are essential to determine how much product you need and how profitable the product line will be. To figure this out, you have to know two critical bits of info: Cost & Margin.

Know your hard cost for manufacturing - what exactly does it cost you to purchase a unit from your supplier - watch out for varying costs from your supplier or external fees charged on one-time bases. If this is not all captured in the correct financial column, a real disappointment lies ahead for you.

Payroll/Overheads - make sure you understand the impact here. Overheads can quickly increase, leaving you without any profit margin. Please beware of the miscellaneous category. It may seem like a waste of time to categorize expenses, but knowing where your money is going out will make a difference in your success.

All expenses are critical to know before you can establish your sales price. Assess your competition's sales price thoroughly; how will you be competitive in the marketplace? What is the highest dollar consumers will pay? The difference between your cost and your sales price is your profit. If you miscalculate your gross margin, financial ruin is probable. Once you have signed contracts with either retailers or a landlord, there is no turning back. Calculating gross margin is tricky; seek out a reliable cost accountant if you aren't sure how to determine what it is.

By now, a sales price should have been established; the last bit is to determine how much gold you can take home at the end of the day and how many units you can move. We strongly suggest breaking this down to realistic numbers; if you are B2C and selling out of a local store, don't calculate how many units you will sell by using national sales numbers! Be wise; who are your friends and neighbors that will buy it? If you live in a major metropolitan area like LA or Dallas, don't expect people two hours away from you to buy in the first year. Be conservative and manage expectations. Better to sell more than projected and miss the numbers on the positive side versus missing on the negative. Some people will tell you this is called "sang-bagging" your numbers; to them, I say it is better to make a profit than not.

There are dangers here, and your first year is critical; the balance between stock levels and not running out requires an amazing amount of focus. It is a constant check and balance routine.

So you establish how many you plan to sell, know the cost of running your business, and determine how profitable you will be with a few simple calculations. Your projections should be clear and easy to explain when asked. The Bottom Line of it all? Will you make any money? If you apply the basics outlined in this book, you should easily find success and earn a nice profit.

★ Profitability

How do you decide if you are profitable? Basic accounting says revenue minus expenses equals profits. In basic business terms, this is a correct statement.

Please consider your giving back to the community as a part of that equation. Just as important as having a goal to achieve success, your mission should include helping others.

Yes, your investors want you to make money so everyone can share in the fruits of the labor. In my opinion, the sweetest fruit of labor is to give back. I strongly encourage you to make it a part of your mission statement to support those less fortunate. In addition to treating your employees well and fair and equal pay practices, collectively find a non-profit group that needs funding. Get your employees involved, and designate a portion of your profits for a charitable cause. Doing this provides higher profitability than just what leftover after you pay the bills. It helps the world be a better place. And that, my friends, is the greatest wealth that can be obtained.

Sales

So it all comes down to this, Sales. With all the pieces of the puzzle adequately interlocked for your business and the product itself, success won't occur without that projection of sales happening. All the planning and forecasting in the world is a beautiful tool, but it doesn't equate to a person actually buying your product. Great marketing only opens the opportunity - making you and your team drive the sale; this is how you prove success.

If you are working on a B2B situation, you will still need to make sales calls. Your customer is your outfacing vendor who will ultimately place the product in a consumer's hands. The sales function doesn't require any less work in a B2B than it does in a B2C; it's just a different approach. Your sales team is a critical part of your business, and if you plan to make sales and manage the supply chain, plan to reduce the number of hours you sleep.

My approach to sales is two-fold - the use of inside and outside sales. First, let's talk about outside sales; this is the person out shaking hands at trade shows, making the big pitch at the retailers' meeting, and meeting people who need to know about the product line. Inside sales are meant to be a support system, employees who are every bit as capable as outside sales but have the ability to anticipate and support the needs of the person in the field. As your business grows, clearly define these roles and be transparent with team members about what their responsibilities are. Define those boundaries!

If I am sitting in your chair, I am thinking, why is he bringing up a sales force when I am just a small product company? The reason is quite simple, to encourage you to plan ahead. If you anticipate these human costs early on, you won't impact your company's profitability as you expand. One could argue that as my sales grow, my COGs will reduce, and I can offset the human resources cost. That is certainly possible; however, entertain the thought that the product line will have a better opportunity for longevity if you plan for it now. I have seen it first hand; people want raises, landlords raise the rent, and suppliers increase their prices; the impact of this will seriously erode your margins if you have not adequately planned sales costs.

Good salespeople need to receive incentives, and by that, I am saying they need a clear-cut path to know their earning potential. For a dedicated salesperson, a pat on the back is great, but a check in the bank is better. Do both; your team will work endlessly to make you all winners.

Put strong controls in place to manage what outward messages are presented. Don't be shy to reign in a salesperson who makes stuff up. At the end of the day, it is your company's reputation, and you must protect it. The flip side is to make sure your sales department is given the tools and support they need to function correctly.

Information-Information-Information.

Use all means necessary to ensure your branding is consistent across all members of the team. Everyone must carry the same face forward; if the message is misaligned, quickly figure out where it is and resolve it. If it means termination, then remove the challenge. Just make sure your actions match the core values of the company.

Define a transparent pay structure for your company; every employee needs a plan for success. Even if it's only two of you, define roles and compensation clearly from the beginning. Put your strategies to work and avoid missing expectations (real or imagined). The input lets you ensure you plan your expenses correctly so you properly manage profitability. Don't expect to work without a salary either; most any lender or investor will require you clearly define your salary. It is not a solid business practice to live off the profits as they occur.

What's the difference between revenue and profit? I mention this as it is essential you understand the difference and are cautious about what numbers you present externally. First off, if you are a privately held company (not publicly traded), it is no one's business how much money you make. The exception, of course, is your investors and appropriate government agencies; these entities will need to know how much money you made in the past X months. It is, however, critical that you show growth in your company to potential sales partners. When speaking to outsiders, the recommendation is to use revenue growth percentages, year over year, to establish a growth pattern. Your end customers don't need to know this, but some will place value on your brand based on your growth scale. Develop an ingenious and yet clever way to provide that info. Don't become concerned with this comes up; answer the question in a way that shows growth without revealing the business' profitability.

People often want to share details unnecessarily to prove a point; be wary of doing that. Too much information in the wrong hands can create unnecessary chaos for you.

That's a wrap

You have been presented with what I have learned throughout my career. Based on my years of experience, the info contained herein is what I deem as the basics to launch a product line.

In the end, more involved transactions than what I have written about will occur; this book intends to give you key takeaways to utilize as you plan your adventure. It is incredibly thrilling to witness the number of people living out their dreams by taking this task on. Yes, it was work with stress piled on top, but at the end of the day, people who have traveled the road believed in what they were chasing and had a great time along the way.

We didn't touch on ingestible or oral products; although many of the practices listed herein would apply, ingestible/oral products are not my area of expertise. I would be remiss in offering advice on the ins and outs of a business model I do not know in detail.

Have a strong business plan in place. If you haven't taken the time to understand how to achieve your dream, it will always lie just beyond your grasp. As I like to say - A plan without a due date is merely a conversation.

So build a plan, understand the dynamics around getting there, and then run like hell!

Now back to the brand mentioned early on.

The lack of knowledge and learning curves they ran into were costly. The owners clearly defined the vision, but not everyone in the organization bought into the concept. Without this support internally, the product ambled along for a few years. The products were excellent and created by a world-renowned formulator; however, in the end, that wasn't enough. Leadership didn't have a healthy enough game plan in place and didn't hire the correct people to drive the bus. The most significant learning curve, and ultimately what hurt the business, was a lack of clear understanding of ownership and exclusivity.

Although we didn't touch on ownership in-depth, have a good lawyer on your team, and be clear about who owns the brand name and the product line itself. A quality manufacturer will have a well-written contract that is mutually protective of both parties. It is my opinion agreements that are one-sided in their approach don't fall under the guise of partnership. The manufacturer must protect their interest, as do you; it is possible to meet on an even plane with everyone feeling whole at the end of the day.

Many companies offer what is known as Private Label (PL) products. These are generic product lines that serve a purpose and are great if all you are concerned with is having an EGO brand.

(Your name on the packaging.) There is nothing wrong with this path while establishing a name while you look to the future. Just know you will not own any rights to the product and will always be at the manufacturer's mercy. If they change something or cancel it, there will be little you can do about it. Be cautious about PL and the option for customizing products; while this may seem a great way to differentiate the product line on your shelf, you will have no ownership of the products. This makes an acquisition of the product line in the future virtually nil. One caveat I will share is; if you want to enhance your overall business for acquisition, PL may significantly enhance revenue and client loyalty.

You are feeling incredibly proud at this moment, and you should as much effort has gone into getting this far. Don't lose your feeling of pride when obstacles occur and you are struggling. Decipher what was wrong and recalculate; owning a brand is a constant search and discovery process. Some things will work better than others; some things you weren't excited about will explode and surprise you. It's all part of the journey.

Time will not be your friend; utilize an active project manager who understands timelines and reiterations. Delays are inevitable, but it is not an end to the project. Allow for it upfront, add some cushion into your commitments, and be clear on your suppliers' responsibilities for not meeting deadlines. A substantial penalty is an excellent motivator for manufacturers and a great tool for the executive levels in a company to know failures are present in their systems. Nothing travels faster to the corner office than the CFO losing money because someone dropped the ball.

Good luck with your adventure. I take great pride in passing along the information I have captured over the years. I intend to assist others in following their passion and taking their product into the marketplace.

Thadeus Parkland

If you would like additional insights or guidance for your project, you may reach Thadeus Parkland through P1Press.

Various programs are available to assist you in taking your product to market.

Thadeus Parkland is not affiliated with any manufacturing company nor does he receive any compensation for vendor recommendations.

Other titles available through P1Press are:

Ready To Own A Salon? 10 Things You Should Know

Deathbed Confession: My Son Was A Stolen Baby!

The Girl Who Stole My Chair!

My Life Being A Sensitive

P1Press

ISBN 978-1-7329729-5-7

9 781732 972957

90000